Erstes Englisch
mit Billy Malone

Billy at home

Zu Hause • Essen und Trinken • Freizeit

TESSLOFF

Foreword
Vorwort

Herzlich willkommen in der Welt von Billy Malone!
Auf den nächsten Seiten begegnest du Billy, seiner Familie und seinem kleinen Hund Charly. Die Familie Malone begleitet dich bei deinen ersten Schritten in der englischen Sprache.
In lustigen Bildergeschichten und einfachen Sätzen erfährst du, was Billy zu Hause alles erlebt. Anhand von vielen leichten Aufgaben lernst du deine ersten englischen Wörter und festigst deinen Wortschatz.

Am besten lernst du Englisch, wenn du so viel wie möglich sprichst! Lass dir die englischen Wörter von jemandem vorlesen, der Englisch kann, damit du dir gleich die richtige Aussprache einprägst. Die Bildergeschichten kannst du dir auch im Internet auf **www.tessloff.com** anhören.

Damit man genau weiß, wie die Wörter ausgesprochen werden, gibt es die so genannte Lautschrift. Sie benutzt bestimmte Zeichen, die immer für einen ganz bestimmten Laut stehen. Im Vokabelverzeichnis am Ende des Heftes findest du hinter jedem englischen Wort auch die dazugehörige Lautschrift.

Dies sind die wichtigsten Zeichen:

ɑː wie in lahm
iː wie in Biene
uː wie in Blume
i wie in Baby
ɪ wie in Kiste
e wie in Bett
æ ähnlich wie in Bär
ʌ wie in Kamm
ɒ wie in Motte
ə wie in Mitte
ʊ wie in Butter

aɪ wie in Mai
ɔɪ wie in Eule
aʊ wie in Haus
eə ähnlich wie in leer
ɪə wie in Tier
ɜː ähnlich wie in hört
ʤ wie in Dschungel
ʒ wie in Garage
ŋ wie in Ring
ʃ wie in Schlange
ʧ wie in tschüss

v wie in Vase
z wie in Sonne
s wie in Messer

Diese Laute gibt es nur in Englisch:

θ wie in think
ð wie in this
w wie in water
r wie in red
eɪ wie in day
əʊ wie in low

The Malones, Billy's family

Die Malones, Billys Familie

Herzlich willkommen bei den Malones!
Billy Malone ist 10 Jahre alt. Er wohnt mit seinen Eltern Mary und Peter und seinen beiden Schwestern Sally und Susan in einem hübschen Haus in einer kleinen Stadt in England.
Zur Familie gehören außerdem noch Oma Laura und Opa Joe, Onkel Tom und Tante Claire mit ihren beiden Kindern Peggy und Ron.
Ach ja, da fehlt ja noch einer: Natürlich gehört Charly auch zur Familie! Charly ist der kleine Hund der Malones und Billys bester Freund.

Ghosts in the house

Gespenster im Haus

Es ist Samstagabend und Billy und Sally sind allein zu Hause. Sie sind im Wohnzimmer und schauen einen Film im Fernsehen.

Schau dir die Bilder an. Weißt du, wie die Geschichte weitergeht? Versuche dann, die englischen Sätze zu lesen und zu verstehen.

Billy and Sally are alone at home. They are watching television.

Billy says, “Can you hear that noise, Sally?”

Sally answers, “Yes, I can. Do you think it’s a ghost?”

Billy: “No, I don’t think so. Where is the noise coming from?”

Billy looks into his parents' bedroom.
But there is no ghost.

He looks into the bathroom.
But there is no ghost.

Suddenly Billy hears the noise
again. It is coming from the attic!

Billy laughs. "Here is your ghost, Sally!
What sweet ghosts!"

Billy's words

alone – allein
at home – zu Hause
to hear – hören
noise – Geräusch
to answer – antworten
to think – denken
to come from – herkommen
again – nochmal, wieder
suddenly – plötzlich
sweet – süß, niedlich

The Malones' house

Das Haus der Malones

Hier siehst du das Haus, in dem die Familie Malone wohnt.

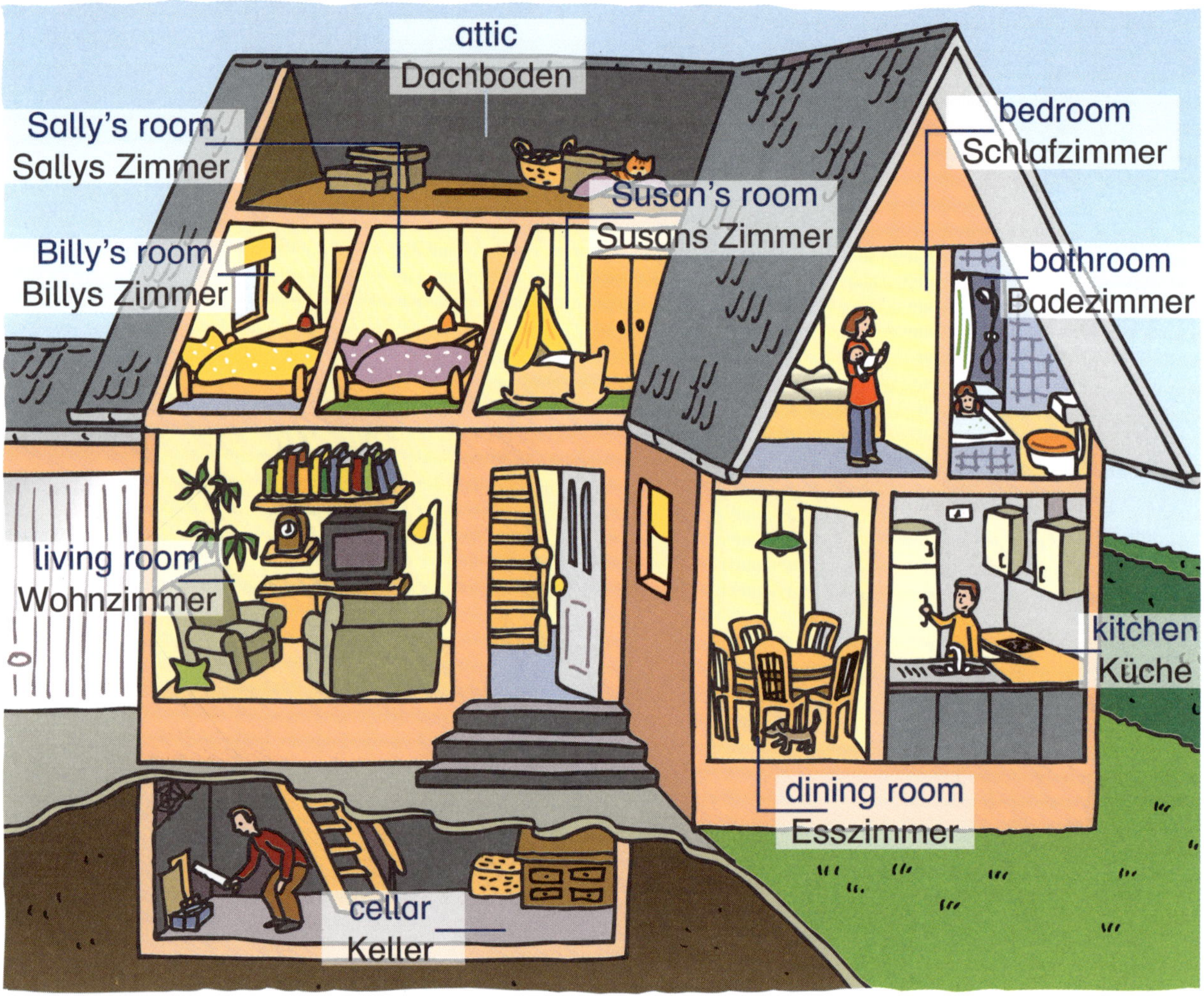

Fill in the right words!
Trage die richtigen Wörter ein!

Billy is in the . . . .

Sally is in the . . . .

Charly is in the . . . .

Mr Malone is in the . . . .

Mrs Malone is in the . . . .

Susan is in the . . . . , too.

armchair
Sessel

sofa
Sofa

bed
Bett

shower
Dusche

bath
Badewanne

toilet
Toilette

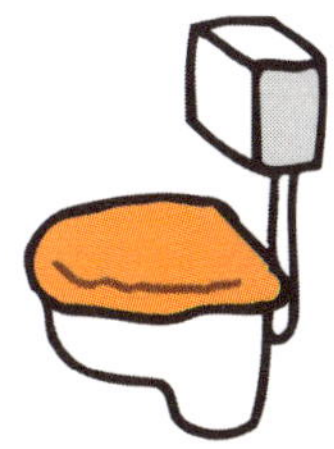

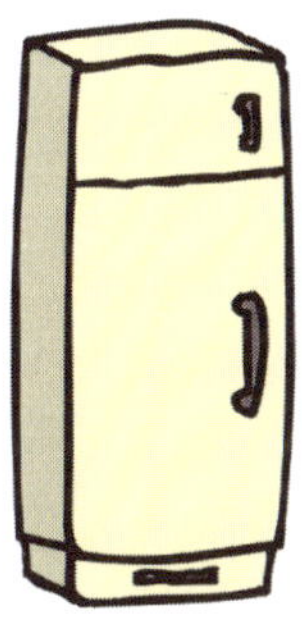

fridge
Kühlschrank

wardrobe
Schrank

Mark the right answer with a cross!
Kreuze die richtige Antwort an!

In the kitchen there is

☐ a sofa ☐ a bed ☐ a fridge

In the bedroom you can find

☐ a wardrobe ☐ a shower ☐ a toilet

The bath is

☐ in the attic ☐ in Billy’s room ☐ in the bathroom

The armchair is in

☐ the living room ☐ the kitchen ☐ the cellar

Find the words and put them in the right place!

Finde die Wörter und beschrifte die Teile des Hauses.

DACHRINNEGUTTERTÜRDOORAUTOCARTREPPESTAIRS

HAUSHOUSEFENSTERWINDOWDACHROOF

BALKONBALCONYSCHORNSTEINCHIMNEY

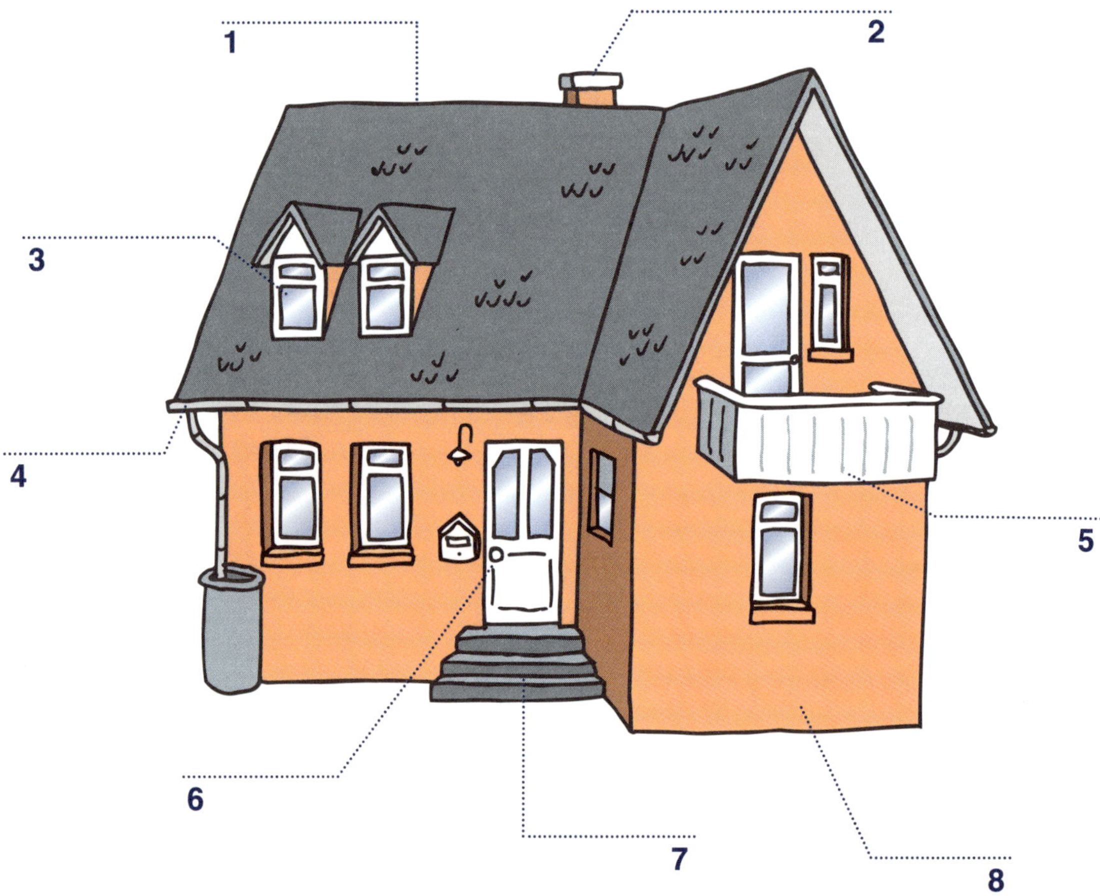

One word doesn't belong to the house. Draw it here!

Ein Wort bleibt übrig. Es gehört nicht zum Haus. Male es hier hin!

Do the crossword!

Löse das Kreuzworträtsel!

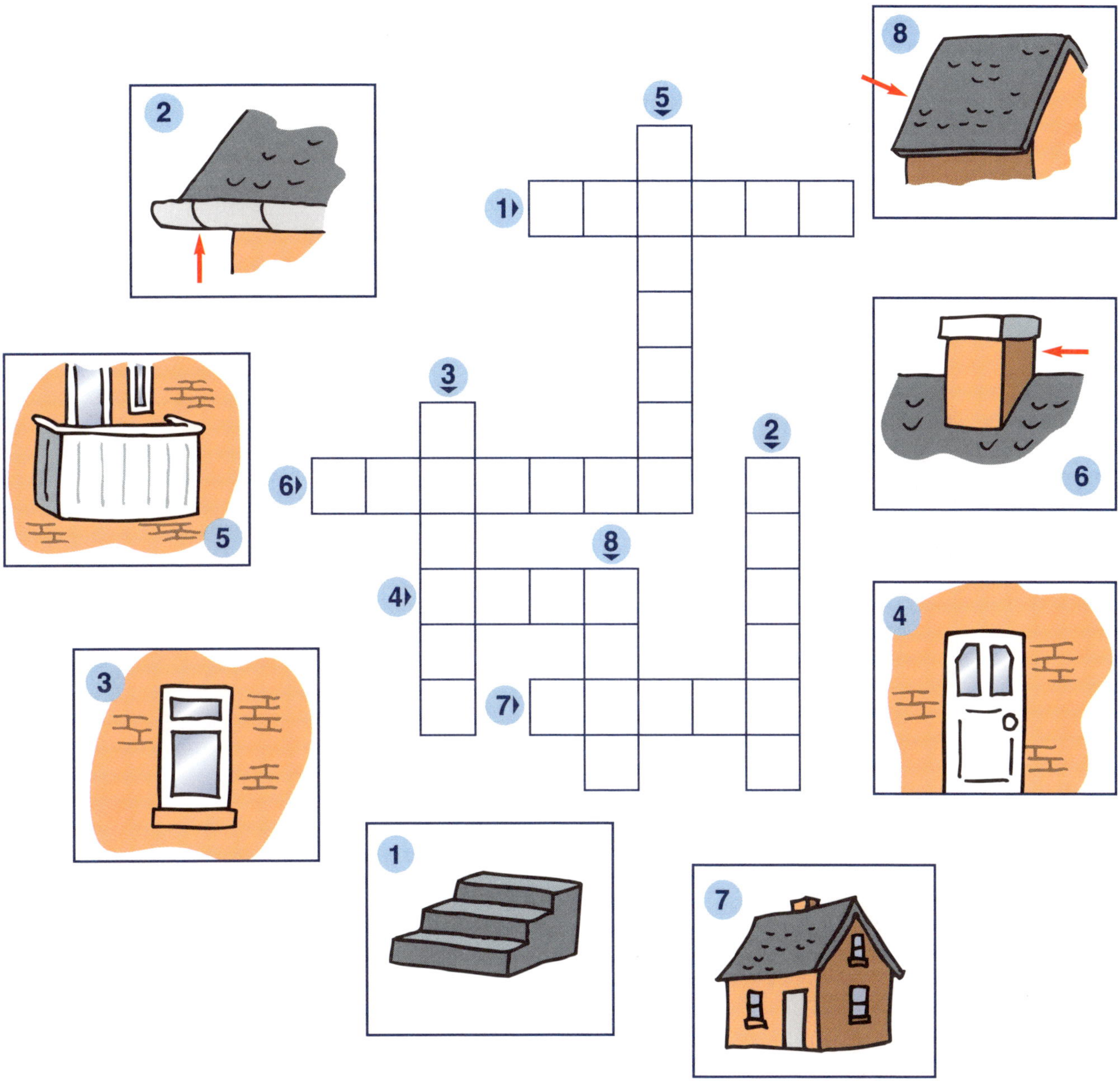

Make sentences!

Bilde Sätze!

Show me the roof, please!
Zeig mir bitte das Dach!

This is the roof.
Dies ist das Dach!

Show me . . . .

This is . . . .

Charly's favourite food

Charlys Lieblingsessen

Mrs Malone bereitet das Abendessen zu. Heute gibt es Würstchen, Billys Lieblingsessen. Billy und Sally decken den Tisch.

Schau dir die Bilder an. Weißt du, wie die Geschichte weitergeht? Versuche dann, die englischen Sätze zu lesen und zu verstehen.

Billy and Sally lay the table for dinner.

Mrs Malone brings sausages. Billy is happy. He likes sausages.

Charly is hungry, too. Billy says, "No, Charly, not my sausages!"

"Where is Daddy?" thinks Mrs Malone. They start eating.

"Stop it, Charly! You must wait for your dog biscuits," says Sally.

Charly is sad. Sausages are his favourite food.

Suddenly Mr Malone comes in. Billy turns around. "Hello, Daddy!" he says.

Oh no! Charly jumps – and now he has got Billy's sausage in his mouth!

Billy's words

to lay the table – den Tisch decken
happy – glücklich
to like – mögen
hungry – hungrig
today – heute
where is – wo ist
to wait – warten
dog biscuits – Hundekuchen
favourite food – Lieblingsessen
to turn around – sich umdrehen
to jump – springen
mouth – Mund, Maul

Food

Lebensmittel

In Mrs Malones Küche sind noch mehr leckere Dinge zum Essen und Trinken.

Write the German words under the pictures!
Schreibe die deutschen Wörter unter die Bilder!

	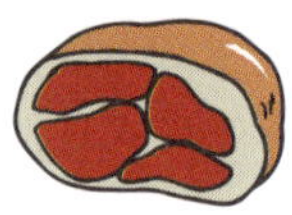		
cheese	ham	butter	bread

milk	eggs	cake	soup

chicken	potatoes	tomatoes	chocolate

Make sentences!
Bilde Sätze!

My favourite food is chicken.
Mein Lieblingsessen ist Hähnchen.

I don't like potatoes.
Ich mag keine Kartoffeln.

My ....

....

I don't like ....

....

My ....

....

I don't like ....

....

Fruit or vegetables? Make two lists!

Obst oder Gemüse? Fülle die Tabelle richtig aus!

lemon

strawberry

peas

peach

mushrooms

apple

plums

lettuce

cauliflower

orange

beans

red pepper

sweet-corn

potatoes

onion

tomatoes

cherries

grapes

fruit	vegetables

watermelon

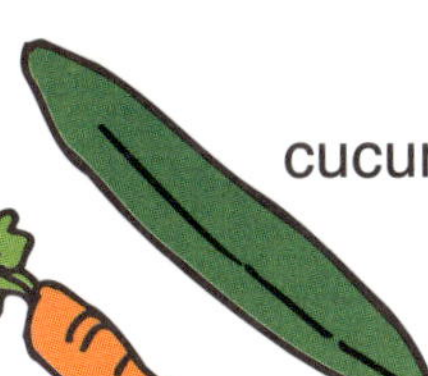
cucumber

carrot

pear

pineapple

banana

Make sentences!
Bilde Sätze!

Billy has porridge and toast for breakfast.
Billy isst Haferbrei und Toast zum Frühstück.

Sally has . . . . for lunch.

Mr Malone has . . . .

Nach dem Essen räumen die Kinder die Küche auf.
Dabei begegnen sie diesen Dingen:

1 cup	2 plate	3 knife	4 glass
5 toaster	6 spoon	7 bowl	8 fork
9 pot	10 bottle	11 pan	12 saucer

Fill in the right words!
Trage die Wörter in die Wortrahmen ein!

Charly's new toy

Charlys neues Spielzeug

Mrs Malone schickt Billy auf den Markt, um frischen Salat für das Abendessen einzukaufen. Charly soll ihn begleiten. Der möchte aber viel lieber spielen...

Schau dir die Bilder an. Weißt du, wie die Geschichte weitergeht? Versuche dann, die englischen Sätze zu lesen und zu verstehen.

"Can you go to the market, please, Billy? I need lettuce for dinner".

"Sorry, Charly, no time to play now. We must go shopping."

Billy buys lettuce. Charly looks for a toy. He wants to play.

"No, Charly! Those are watermelons", Billy says. "You can't play with them."

"Silly dog! Those are grapefruit. You can't play with them!"

Billy and Charly go home. Charly is sad. He hasn't got a toy.

Suddenly Charly wags his tail. There is an old ball under the hedge!

"All right, Charly!" Billy laughs. "Let's play football in the garden now."

Billy's words

dinner – Abendessen
sorry – tut mir leid
market – Markt
to need – brauchen
lettuce – Salat
no time – keine Zeit
to go shopping – einkaufen gehen
to buy – kaufen
to play – spielen
silly dog – dummer Hund
toy – Spielzeug
all right – in Ordnung
to wag the tail – mit dem Schwanz wedeln

In the children's room

Im Kinderzimmer

Stolz trägt Charly seinen neuen Ball ins Kinderzimmer. Dort sind noch andere Spielsachen. Kennst du die Wörter und ihre Bedeutung? Wenn nicht, helfen dir die Malones unten auf der Seite.

Read the words and draw the pictures!
Lies die Wörter und male die Bilder in die Kästchen!

police car
teddy bear
book
ball
puppet

Hier siehst du Billys, Sallys, Susans und Charlys Spielzeug. Wer hat die großen, wer die kleinen Spielsachen?

Big or small? Make sentences.
Groß oder klein? Bilde Sätze.

Charly's ball is big.

Susan's ball is small.

Sally's kite is . . . .

Billy's kite is . . . .

Billy's . . . . is . . . .

. . . .

Do you know what the things in Sally's cupboard are called?

Kennst du all diese Gegenstände in Sallys Schrank?

Left or right? Make sentences!

Links oder rechts? Bilde Sätze!

On the left there is Sally's doll.
Links ist Sallys Puppe.

On the right I can see Sally's hat.
Rechts kann ich Sallys Hut sehen.

On the left . . . .

On the right . . . .

Vocabulary

Vokabeln

A

again [ə'gen]	wieder
all right [ɔ:l'raɪt]	in Ordnung
alone [ə'ləʊn]	allein
and [ænd, ənd]	und
to answer ['ɑ:nsə]	antworten
apple ['æpl]	Apfel
armchair ['ɑ:mtʃeə]	Sessel
at home [ət 'həʊm]	zu Hause
attic ['ætɪk]	Dachboden
aunt [ɑ:nt]	Tante

B

baby ['beɪbi]	Baby
bag [bæg]	Tasche
baked beans [ˌbeɪkt 'bi:nz]	gebackene Bohnen
balcony ['bælkəni]	Balkon
ball [bɔ:l]	Ball
banana [bə'nɑ:nə]	Banane
bath [bɑ:θ]	Badewanne
bathroom ['bɑ:θrʊm]	Badezimmer
bean [bi:n]	Bohne
bed [bed]	Bett
bedroom ['bedrʊm]	Schlafzimmer
big [bɪg]	groß
biscuit ['bɪskɪt]	Keks
book [bʊk]	Buch
bottle ['bɒtl]	Flasche
bowl [bəʊl]	Schüssel
bread [bred]	Brot
breakfast ['brekfəst]	Frühstück
to bring [brɪŋ]	bringen
butter ['bʌtə]	Butter
to buy [baɪ]	kaufen

C

cake [keɪk]	Kuchen
can [kæn]	können
candle ['kændl]	Kerze
car [kɑ:]	Auto
carrot ['kærət]	Möhre, Karotte
cauliflower ['kɒlɪflaʊə]	Blumenkohl
cellar ['selə]	Keller
cherry ['tʃeri]	Kirsche
cheese ['tʃi:z]	Käse
chicken ['tʃɪkɪn]	Hähnchen
child, children [tʃaɪld], ['tʃɪldrən]	Kind, Kinder
children's room ['tʃɪldrənz ˌru:m]	Kinderzimmer
chimney ['tʃɪmni]	Schornstein
chocolate ['tʃɒklət]	Schokolade
clock [klɒk]	Uhr
to come in ['kʌm ɪn]	hereinkommen
to come from ['kʌm frəm]	herkommen
cousin ['kʌzn]	Cousin, Cousine
cucumber ['kju:kʌmbə]	Gurke
cup [kʌp]	Tasse
cupboard ['kʌbəd]	Schrank

D

dining room ['daɪnɪŋrʊm]	Esszimmer
dinner ['dɪnə]	Abendessen
dog [dɒg]	Hund
dog biscuits ['dɒgˌbɪskɪts]	Hundekuchen
doll [dɒl]	Puppe
door [dɔ:]	Tür

E

to eat [i:t]	essen
egg [eg]	Ei

F

family ['fæmɪli]	Familie
father ['fɑ:ðə]	Vater
favourite food [ˌfeɪvərɪt 'fu:d]	Lieblingsessen
to find [faɪnd]	finden
food [fu:d]	Lebensmittel
football ['fʊtbɔ:l]	Fußball
fork [fɔ:k]	Gabel
fridge [frɪdʒ]	Kühlschrank
fried potatoes [fraɪd pə'teɪtəʊz]	Bratkartoffeln
fruit [fru:t]	Obst

G

garden ['gɑ:dn]	Garten
ghost [gəʊst]	Gespenst, Geist
glass [glɑ:s]	Glas
to go shopping [ˌgəʊ 'ʃɒpɪŋ]	einkaufen
grandfather ['grændˌfɑ:ðə]	Großvater
grandmother ['grændˌmʌðə]	Großmutter
grape [greɪp]	Weintraube
grapefruit ['greɪpfru:t]	Pampelmuse
gutter ['gʌtə]	Dachrinne

H

ham [hæm]	Schinken
happy ['hæpi]	glücklich
hat [hæt]	Hut
he [hi:]	er
to hear [hɪə]	hören
hedge [hedʒ]	Hecke
here [hɪə]	hier
house [haʊs]	Haus
hungry ['hʌŋgri]	hungrig

I

I [aɪ]	ich
in [ɪn]	in
into ['ɪntə, 'ɪntu:]	in (hinein)
it [ɪt]	es

J

to jump [dʒʌmp]	springen

K

kitchen ['kɪtʃɪn]	Küche
kite [kaɪt]	Drachen
knife [naɪf]	Messer

L

lamp [læmp]	Lampe
to laugh [lɑ:f]	lachen
to lay the table [ˌleɪ ðə 'teɪbl]	den Tisch decken
left [left]	links
lemon ['lemən]	Zitrone
lettuce ['letɪs]	Salat
to like [laɪk]	mögen
living room ['lɪvɪŋrʊm]	Wohnzimmer
to look [lʊk]	schauen
to look for ['lʊk fɔ:]	suchen
lunch [lʌntʃ]	Mittagessen

M

market ['mɑ:kɪt]	Markt
milk [mɪlk]	Milch
mirror ['mɪrə]	Spiegel
mother ['mʌðə]	Mutter
mouth [maʊθ]	Mund, Maul
mushroom ['mʌʃrʊm]	Pilz
must [mʌst]	müssen
my [maɪ]	mein, meine

N

to need [ni:d]	brauchen
new [nju:]	neu
no [nəʊ]	nein, kein
noise [nɔɪz]	Geräusch
not [nɒt]	nicht
now [naʊ]	jetzt

O

old [əʊld]	alt
onion ['ʌnjən]	Zwiebel
orange ['ɒrɪndʒ]	Orange

P

pan [pæn]	Pfanne
parents ['peərənts]	Eltern
pea [pi:]	Erbse
peach [pi:tʃ]	Pfirsich
pear [peə]	Birne
picture ['pɪktʃə]	Bild
pineapple ['paɪnæpl]	Ananas
place [pleɪs]	Platz
plate [pleɪt]	Teller
to play [pleɪ]	spielen
please [pli:z]	bitte
plum [plʌm]	Pflaume
police car [pə'li:sˌkɑ:]	Polizeiauto
porridge ['pɒrɪdʒ]	Haferbrei
pot [pɒt]	Topf

potato [pə'teɪtəʊ]	Kartoffel
puppet ['pʌpɪt]	Marionette

R

radio ['reɪdiəʊ]	Radio
recorder [rɪ'kɔːdə]	Blockflöte
red pepper [ˌred 'pepə]	rote Paprika
right [raɪt]	rechts, richtig
roof [ruːf]	Dach
room [ruːm, rʊm]	Raum, Zimmer

S

sad [sæd]	traurig
salad ['sæləd]	Salat
sandwiches ['sænwɪdʒɪz]	belegte Brote
saucer ['sɔːsə]	Untertasse
sausages ['sɒsɪdʒɪz]	Würstchen
to say [seɪ]	sagen
scrambled eggs [ˌskræmbld 'egz]	Rühreier
to see [siː]	sehen
she [ʃiː]	sie
to show [ʃəʊ]	zeigen
shower ['ʃaʊə]	Dusche
silly ['sɪli]	dumm
sister ['sɪstə]	Schwester
small [smɔːl]	klein
sofa ['səʊfə]	Sofa
sorry ['sɒri]	tut mir leid, Entschuldigung
soup [suːp]	Suppe
spoon [spuːn]	Löffel
stairs [steəz]	Treppe
to start [stɑːt]	anfangen
to stop [stɒp]	aufhören
strawberry ['strɔːbəri]	Erdbeere
suddenly ['sʌdənli]	plötzlich
sweet [swɪːt]	süß, niedlich
sweetcorn ['swɪːtkɔːn]	Mais

T

tea [tiː]	Tee
teatime ['tiːtaɪm]	Tee (Mahlzeit am Nachmittag)
teddy bear ['tediˌbeə]	Teddy
thank you ['θæŋk juː]	danke
the [ðə, ði]	der, die, das
there [ðeə]	da, dort
they [ðeɪ]	sie (3. P. Plural)
things [θɪŋz]	Sachen, Dinge
to think [θɪŋk]	denken
time [taɪm]	Zeit
toast [təʊst]	Toast
toaster ['təʊstə]	Toaster
today [tə'deɪ]	heute
toilet ['tɔɪlət]	Toilette
tomato [tə'mɑːtəʊ]	Tomate
too [tuː]	auch
toy [tɔɪ]	Spielzeug
to turn around [ˌtɜːn ə'raʊnd]	sich umdrehen

U

umbrella [ʌm'brelə]	Schirm
uncle ['ʌŋkl]	Onkel
under ['ʌndə]	unter

V

vegetable ['vedʒtəbl]	Gemüse

W

to wag the tail [ˌwæg ðə 'teɪl]	mit dem Schwanz wedeln
to wait [weɪt]	warten
to want [wɒnt]	wollen, möchten
wardrobe ['wɔːdrəʊb]	Kleiderschrank
to watch television [ˌwɒtʃ 'telɪvɪʒən]	fernsehen
watermelon ['wɔːtəˌmelən]	Wassermelone
we [wiː]	wir
where [weə]	wo, woher
window ['wɪndəʊ]	Fenster
word [wɜːd]	Wort

Y

you [juː]	du, ihr, Sie

Solutions

Lösungen

Seite 6

Billy is in the kitchen.
Sally is in the bathroom.
Charly is in the dining room.
Mr Malone is in the cellar.
Mrs Malone is in the bedroom.
Susan is in the bedroom, too.

Seite 7

In the kitchen there is a fridge.
In the bedroom you can find a wardrobe.
The bath is in the bathroom.
The armchair is in the living room.

Seite 8

1 roof
2 chimney
3 window
4 gutter
5 balcony
6 door
7 stairs
8 house

Das Wort **car** bleibt übrig.

Seite 9

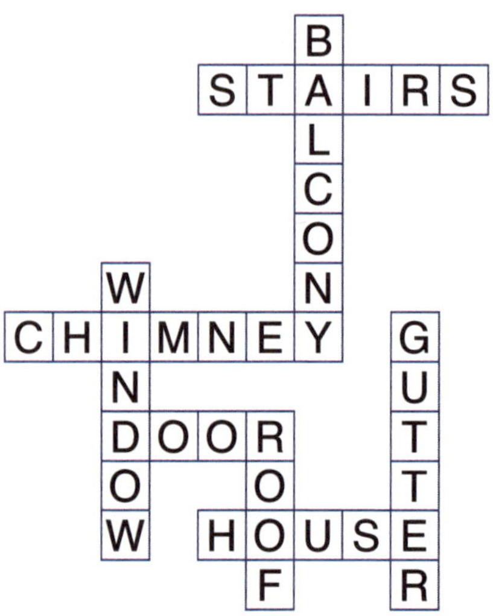

Seite 12

cheese – Käse
ham – Schinken
butter – Butter
bread – Brot
milk – Milch
eggs – Eier
cake – Kuchen
soup – Suppe
chicken – Hähnchen
potatoes – Kartoffeln
tomatoes – Tomaten
chocolate – Schokolade

Seite 13

fruit
strawberry – lemon – apple
orange – cherries – watermelon
pear – pineapple – banana
grapes – plums – peach

vegetables
lettuce – red pepper
sweetcorn – onion – carrot
cucumber – tomatoes
potatoes – beans – cauliflower
mushrooms – peas

Seite 15

toaster, cup
bottle, spoon
fork, bowl
pan, pot
glass, plate
saucer, knife

Seite 18

So gehören die Wörter zusammen:

police car – Polizeiauto
teddy bear – Teddybär
book – Buch
ball – Ball
puppet – Marionette

Seite 19

Sally's kite is small.
Billy's kite is big.
Billy's car is big.
Charly's car is small.
Sally's teddy bear is big.
Susan's teddy bear is small.
Susan's doll is big.
Charly's doll is small.

Seite 20

On the left there is Sally's lamp.
On the right I can see Sally's book.
On the left there is Sally's candle.
On the right I can see Sally's bag.
On the left there is Sally's picture.
On the right I can see Sally's recorder.
On the left there is Sally's clock.
On the right I can see Sally's radio.
On the left there is Sally's mirror.
On the right I can see Sally's umbrella.